NATIONAL GEOGRAPHIC

Where Do You Live?

Harley Chan

My name is Sasha.
I live in the **United States of America**.
The United States of America looks
like this on a map.

CALIFOR

ALASKA

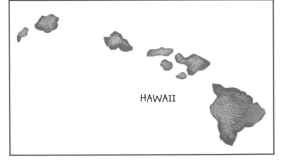

HAWAII

3

I live in the state of **Colorado**.

The state of Colorado looks like this on a map.

COLORADO

I live in the city of **Denver**.

The city of Denver looks like this on a map.

Denver★

COLORADO

I live in Denver, Colorado, in the United States of America.

Denver·
COLORADO

Where do you live?